Chronically in Church

When Church Negatively Impacts Your Relationship with God

Claira Smith

***Priority*ONE**
publications

Detroit, MI USA

Chronically in Church
When Church Negatively Impacts Your Relationship with God
Copyright © 2025 Claira Smith.

Scripture quotations taken from the Amplified® Bible (AMP), Copyright © 2015 by The Lockman Foundation. Used by permission. lockman.org

Scripture quotations from The Authorized (King James) Version. Rights in the Authorized Version in the United Kingdom are vested in the Crown. Reproduced by permission of the Crown's patentee, Cambridge University Press

Scripture quotations taken from the (LSB®) Legacy Standard Bible®, Copyright © 2021 by The Lockman Foundation. Used by permission. All rights reserved. Managed in partnership with Three Sixteen Publishing Inc. LSBible.org and 316publishing.com.

Scripture quotations marked (NIV) are taken from the Holy Bible, New International Version®, NIV®. Copyright © 1973, 1978, 1984, 2011 by Biblica, Inc.™ Used by permission of Zondervan. All rights reserved worldwide. www.zondervan.comThe "NIV" and "New International Version" are trademarks registered in the United States Patent and Trademark Office by Biblica, Inc.™

Scripture quotations marked (NLT) are taken from the *Holy Bible*, New Living Translation, copyright ©1996, 2004, 2015 by Tyndale House Foundation. Used by permission of Tyndale House Publishers, Carol Stream, Illinois 60188. All rights reserved.

All rights reserved. No part of this publication may be reproduced, stored in a retrieval system, or transmitted in any form or by any means – electronic, mechanical, photocopy, recording, or any other – except for brief quotations in printed reviews without the prior permission of the publisher.

*Priority*ONE Publications
P. O. Box 361332 | Grosse Pointe, MI 48236
E-mail: info@priorityonebooks.com
URL: http://www.priorityonebooks.com

PRINT BOOK
ISBN 13:   978-1-933972-74-9
ISBN 10:   1-933972-74-2

EBOOK
ISBN 13:   978-1-933972-75-6
ISBN 10:   1-933972-75-0

Editing by Patricia Hicks
Cover and Interior design by Christina Dixon

Printed in the United States of America

Table of Contents

Chapter One: The Problem as I See It 1

Chapter Two: The Mission of Jesus 7

Chapter Three: Background 13

Chapter Four: Education: How the church taught me to resolve conflict 17

Chapter Five: Marriage, Prosperity, and Being Blessed? 29

Chapter Six: Worship 35

Chapter Seven: Evangelism/Inner Conflict 45

Chapter Eight: Fellowship 53

Chapter Nine: What is the Job of the Church? The Believer? 61

Chapter Ten: Resolution 67

Chapter Eleven: Final Thoughts & Discussion Questions 75

Bibliography 79

Dedication

I dedicate this book to my Heavenly Father,
Whose love for me has provided the guidance
needed to get beyond the misunderstanding that
almost made me miss Him.

Chapter One:
The Problem as I See It

While believers still meet Sunday after Sunday, many of our worship services no longer have the impact they once did. The body of Christ senses it, and society reflects it. If we are passionate about the things of God, there should be a concern about the health of the body of Christ. As with any illness, we have to find the source of the problem to diagnose and treat the issue properly. People, individually and collectively, make up the body of Christ. As such, the church must be willing to examine themselves to obtain a diagnosis. What are we adding positively or negatively to the church and body of Christ as a whole, and how does that affect the cause of Christ? What's my definition of Chronically in Church? My definition is:

> *Continued misuse or misunderstanding of the church's intended function that results in "spiritual illness."*

This definition was at the root of my understanding. So, I was dedicated to going to church. However, my biblically inaccurate understanding of what church was and what it was for was making me spiritually sick, in a sense. According to this Scripture, I was taught on the extreme: "God has given each of you a gift from his great variety of spiritual gifts. Use them well to serve one another." 1 Peter 4:10 NLT.

My training? Serving in the church was the next level of performance as a Christian. Serving in the church was the heart of God. Serving in church was how you got God's attention. If you were not serving in the church, you barely had a relationship with God. My childhood was centered around sacrificing myself for everything and everyone else. That was what it took to be a Christian. That's how I saw the matriarchs in my family life, so as far as I was concerned, it had to be right.

Picture this. I stood in the sanctuary, and she walked past me like I didn't exist. If she could, she would have walked through me. I thought maybe it's just me. I'm overthinking it. At the next service

I made it my mission to make sure I spoke. I saw her, and with all the excitement I could muster, "Oh my gosh, Hey sis, you cute!" She momentarily stopped mid-step, gave a quick thank you, and sat on the other side of the sanctuary. But she told the pastor how rude I was and didn't speak. Another Sunday: "Prophetess, I need you to open us up in prayer." I mounted the pulpit and grabbed the stained microphone. I raised my hand to acknowledge the congregation, and she walked out. Her disdain towards me was apparent to the other members, which started more negative discourse. I asked the pastor if I should talk to her. "Well, Claira," he said, "You do have a habit of…" going on to list everything I needed to work on to be a better minister and love people better. He described how I was never disrespectful, but I could be nicer. God said it was time to move on. I spoke with my leader, and he told me God didn't tell him that, so that's not right. In another instance, my then-pastor gave me his blessing, but other members later accused me of planning to sabotage the church. Me? I was simply doing my best to serve.

They used to say the walls have ears, so watch what you say because someone will always hear you. The thing about whispers is that they never stay a whisper. Unfortunately, in my case, it always got back to me. According to the whisperers, my attitude was nasty; she never heard from God; Claira was being shady when she complimented me; she thinks she is better than me, and there is nothing genuine about her. The days my character was tarnished because they felt they could do the title or position better than what I was doing currently. I never complained, confronted, or discussed it; I just showed up. Leaders openly applauded my dedication, and in true church fashion, the church publicly applauded and bullied me behind closed doors. It was a never-ending cycle.

One day after an overall great service, I sat in an empty sanctuary trying to take a moment for myself. A few people, including my leaders, came and joined me. We talked, shared our hearts, and I got some much-needed guidance. While I appreciated them allowing that intimate moment, I still was heavy. My chest felt like an elephant was sitting on it. I had a question, but I was hesitant to ask. I told myself I was reluctant because I knew they were tired. They just preached for 45 minutes and prayed for many others, not to mention we kept them after service just to talk. I was going to accept not sharing and keeping my struggles to myself. It was getting late, and everyone needed to get home anyway. But it was circulating in my thoughts, making my head hurt. They discerned the tension coming from me and told me to ask the question. If you know me, you know I stumbled my way through getting this question out, but eventually, I found my wording and asked, "At what point does long-suffering become accepting abuse?".

Unintentionally, we, the people part of the church, have thwarted the purpose of the church. Because the heart behind our actions no longer reflects the cause of Christ, the church is suffering. As we dive into what's wrong, I think it's important to understand the original intent of the creation of the church.

Chapter Two:
The Mission of Jesus

Why did Jesus come? His mission can be summarized in a couple of Scriptures:

John 3:16—*For God so loved the world, that he gave his only begotten Son, that whosoever believeth in him should not perish but have everlasting life.*

And Luke 19:10, *For the Son of Man came to seek and to save the lost.*

Due to the sin of Adam, humankind was disconnected from God, and that affected every generation, even after the death of Adam. Man did what they could to maintain a connection to God or correct the mistake of Adam through sacrifices of animals and strict adherence to rules (the commandments, etc.), but in all their doing, it was not enough. God accepted their trying, but it was a temporary solution to a deeper problem. God, our Father, knew and understood that we could not save ourselves, so He sent His son Jesus as the ultimate sacrifice. For three years, Jesus (son of God AND God manifested in human form) taught about God and His love for us, performed miracles, healed the sick, etc. During Jesus' ministry, He recruited 12 disciples (students, followers, etc.) to impart His knowledge and train [Matthew 4:18–22, Mark 1:16-20 and Luke 5:1–11]. Because the lessons Jesus taught often challenged the theology of the religious leaders, the Pharisees executed a plan to have Jesus killed (crucified). Jesus was beaten and hung on the cross, where He then gave His life as the ultimate sacrifice. Jesus did what animal sacrifices couldn't do. He became the perfect sacrifice. Animal sacrifices were needed for every single sin for every single person. It was not a sustainable solution. Jesus (100% God) never sinned, so Jesus (also 100% man) became the perfect sacrifice (2 Corinthians 5:21). After three days, Jesus' body could not be found. He had risen as He told His disciples He would in Mark 9: 31. He said to them, "...The Son of Man is going to be delivered into the hands of men. They will kill him, and after three days, he will rise." The disciples Jesus trained were the ones who would continue to teach Jesus' message, the gospel. Eventually, this was the start of the Christian church.

The birth of the Christian church started in the Book of Acts. Before there was a "church," there were 12 disciples following Christ. After the death of Christ, the disciples were instructed not to leave Jerusalem until they were given the gift of the Holy Spirit. For 40 days, they gathered and waited. When they were baptized in the Spirit and given the gift of the Holy Spirit, they began to speak in different languages. People from 15 different regions heard and understood the miracles of Jesus in their own language. The disciples initially only spoke Aramaic. This is what the church calls Pentecost. After the miracle of being baptized in the Holy Spirit, the Apostle Peter preached a sermon that convicted the hearts of about three thousand people. Those people embraced the teaching of Peter, repented, and were baptized. This was the start of the church. The people who chose to believe the teachings of the apostles came together and created an impactful community that was continuously growing. From this brief description of the founding of the church, we find that a successful church has four main components: worship/prayer, education, fellowship, and evangelism. Being a part of the Christian community meant they believed in and applied what they were taught. I can listen to someone talk, but if I don't trust what they're saying, it's going in one ear and out the other. My mentors are at a place in life that I aspire to get to. So, when they speak, I listen and take notes. I apply what they say not to become them but to get to their level, understand things from a different perspective than my own, and hopefully succeed at pleasing God and fulfilling the mission of Christ.

FYI, a good mentor will want you to surpass them. Jesus said in John 14:12 *Verily, verily, I say unto you, He that believeth on me, the works that I do shall he do also; and greater works than these shall he do.* Those from the early Christian church agreed with the apostolic teaching, so they listened, studied, took notes, and lived out the lessons. They poured back into the community that was being built. They heard a literal life-changing message, and it was reflected in their daily lives. From there, they created a community that helped one another and sold their belongings to help the poor. They often ate together, went to the temple together, and encouraged one another. They were intentional and passionate about the mission of Christ. They didn't just hold on to the teachings of the disciples/Apostles; they learned and went out to continue to spread those same teachings, creating new converts. The early Christians were grateful, excited even about their transformation, and passionate about the cause and mission of Christ. They believed in what they were being taught, so they generously passed that message on to all who would listen. Intentional with their community, the doctrine they were dedicated to was reflected in how they interacted with one another. Consistently ensuring that in all their doing, God was always glorified. If they didn't, well, remember Ananias and Sapphira.

Chapter Three:
Background

I've been a part of four churches in my 31 years, three of which were before I turned 18. I grew up Pentecostal, but the type of church I was a member of varied. I have experienced churches in various capacities: storefront, small and mega, just starting or established, strict/traditional, and modern. But I always ran into a similar problem: I needed help understanding why I was going. It was something I knew I was supposed to do, but its purpose was lost to me. I didn't know what it was for, so whatever they told me was what I held on to and lived by. When people ask what my childhood was like, I usually say it was a maturing Christian home, which should be true for every believer. No one person is perfect, no matter how amazing they are. Christ is continually pruning, perfecting, and maturing all of us. People operate at their level of understanding, and once they are informed differently, they change, correct, and do better. So, I could never fault my mother or grandmother for how they raised me. After all, their teaching was vital to my foundation as a believer in Christ. We all were learning and growing together. A lot of the "traditional" childhood was sacrificed in the name of obedience and having a relationship with God. While other children were choreographing dances to Grammy-winning artist Ciara's hit song, *1, 2 Step*, I was focused on speaking in tongues and memorizing Psalms 23. To provide a little more context, if the doors of the church were open, I was expected to be inside the church house.

Because my mother and grandmother were dedicated church members, there was 72-hour prayer, vacation Bible school, holiday rehearsal, and services, the Sundays where the choir had to sing, so I was in more than three services that day, revivals, New Year's, support the pastors' speaking engagements and for all the different types of services the church encourages attendance. We were the first in the building and the last to leave. Staying in certain services until well after midnight during the school week *because the Spirit was high* was expected, and I still went to school the next morning. My grandmother's favorite quote was, "You have to learn to serve." From that quote, I was expected to fill the spot when it was open and available. I've been an usher, sang in the choir (children and young adults), praise team, altar worker, set up and clean-up crew, finance department administrator, assistant armor bearer, and everything else in between. Church was never just church; it was my second 9-5. Despite the exhaustion I inadvertently experienced, I enjoyed it. Being in the house of God and serving the church helped grow my relationship with God. Even outside of the church *building,* we were in church.

Our family had weekly Bible studies where we took turns teaching a specific Scripture. There were many occasions when the church opened other rooms in the building for the children to do homework; this way, parents could be a part of the service, and kids wouldn't fall behind in their studies. Because church took up a lot of my childhood, a lot of life's lessons came from the church. How I handled life's many ups and downs can be traced back to some form of Scripture or church tradition.

Chapter Four:
Education: How the church taught me to resolve conflict

Romans 12:18 – *If it be possible, as much as in you lieth, be at peace with all men.*

Prayer and servitude were the foundation of my grandmother's relationship with God. She passed those down to us without question. There was an instance where I confided in my grandmother about a girl that was bullying me. I sat and talked about how the young lady tormented me and said cruel things about my appearance, and without missing a beat, my grandmother told me to get on my knees and that we were going to pray for her. In the dimly lit living room, we kneeled on the couch. We clasped our hands together, and she told me to pray. She had me pray for this young lady and the things she was dealing with that caused her to lash out and ultimately that God would bless and heal her from the things that caused her pain. Because Scripture tells us in Matthew 5:44, *"But I say unto you, love your enemies, bless them that curse you, do good to them that hate you and pray for them which despitefully use you and persecute you,"* we prayed for her, according to the words written in Ephesians 3:17-21. While I was praying for her, at some point, my throat got tight, that lump started to form, and my voice began to crack. My grandmother said, "You know why praying for your enemies is hard? Because it goes against our human nature. That's why we have to do it." In reality, I was disappointed and frustrated. Not able to comprehend why someone who made my adolescence hell deserved to know the depths of God's love. Why was there no vindication for me? We prayed for only a few minutes, but when we said amen, my grandmother got up to make dinner, and that was the last time we spoke of her or the bullying.

    Conflict is bound to happen because we are human with different perceptions and understanding. How should we, as Christians, handle conflict? Verses like Romans 12:18, Matthew 5:44, and numerous others have been egregiously misinterpreted, causing Christianity to be linked with passivity. I accepted a life of passivity despite the many stories of Jesus confronting Pharisees when discrediting His deity or instances where salesmen were disrespecting His Father's house. I've sat back and listened to conversations of Christians accepting forms of disrespect and labeling it persecution, and that was essentially a part of our birthright when they accepted Christ as their Lord and Savior. Of course, those lessons followed me into adulthood. As seen in my opening, I continued to face conflict, and my only reaction was to pray. As an active minister in the church and the oldest child, I was taught to withstand whatever came my way.

Acknowledging that I was hurt was almost unheard of. I was taught to consider what pushed them to act the way they did and pray for their healing. *Bible studies* never taught me to hold them accountable for their actions or what it means to have healthy boundaries. In other words, forget your humanity for the sake of Christ's mission. The people need to see Jesus, not your wounds. Expressing a grievance or simply saying you were offended or your feelings were hurt was reduced to complaining, which, according to the Scriptures, was also a sin. My role models for Christianity did not have any conflict resolution skills, let alone know how to apologize properly. Holding other people or myself accountable was a lesson I unfortunately missed.

Growing up in this environment caused me to build walls. I lacked an emotionally safe community. What else could I do? I took the emotions out of the relationship. People could live and treat me how they needed to, and I could maintain my "Christian posture." I did not build relationships with other believers. I didn't love them like Christ commanded, I tolerated them. For many years, I missed out on the many benefits the Christian community offers, such as safety, a sense of belonging, emotional support, resources, etc. With this level of understanding, how can we cultivate a healthy Christian community (church, the institution)? The short answer would be that we can't. Continuing with this level of understanding will push the church as an institution to extinction. *The Washington Post* article: *The Great Dechurching*, looks at why people are leaving churches: 18% of people left the church due to not feeling much love from the congregation, and 15% due to negative experiences. The very people we are called to minister God's love to are being pushed out of the community we say they need.

Of course, a better understanding of Scripture is needed to create a community that can withstand the test of time, but emotional maturity and conflict resolution skills are also vital. From my history with the church, conflict, and its resolution usually looked like apologies that were reduced to a tight embrace while rocking back and forth as the offender spoke in tongues in your ear or what the millennials in my church circle coined as a "Holy Ghost hug."

My belief? The Christian experience is built on relationships. Christ came so that our relationship with God could be mended. It would be foolish to think God doesn't care about the state of our relationships with one another.

How should I handle conflict with another believer? The Bible has many Scriptures on handling conflict or sin against another believer. But the instruction with each verse is to resolve the issue. A more famous one but the least practiced is Matthew 18:15-17 LSB:

> If your brother sins, go and show him his fault in private; if he listens to you, you have won your brother. But if he does not listen to you, take one or two more with you, so that BY THE MOUTH OF TWO OR THREE WITNESSES EVERY FACT MAY BE CONFIRMED. If he refuses to listen to them, tell it to the church, and if he refuses to listen even to the church, let him be to you as a Gentile and a tax collector.

Before we jump to confronting our offender, I think a lot of us would benefit from another step.

> *"A fool gives full vent to his anger, but a wise man keeps himself under control."*
> Proverbs 29:11 NIV

This Scriptural instruction calls believers to control their emotions, not to suppress, ignore, or surrender to them. Controlling our emotions allows us time to better understand what exactly we're upset about or whether it's worth confronting or not. For the passive believer (like me), this requires acknowledging that you've been hurt. I was taught to pray and unintentionally admonished to ignore my emotions in order to maintain a posture of prayer. Because prayer was the right thing to do, and my uncontrolled emotions were still a very real factor, I built walls to protect myself. Experiencing emotions became a bad thing. Living in that condition I suppressed my feelings and stopped being able to recognize my own emotions or the impact of a lack thereof. Unfortunately, the walls I built to protect myself could not differentiate between positive and negative emotions, so it blocked out all of them. Unresolved negative emotions can cause a lot of damage when left unaddressed.

According to the American Psychological Association, consistent chronic stress weakens the immune system. Within relationships, ministry etc. it is imperative that we acknowledge and properly tend to emotional pain. Jesus demonstrated this in multiple instances in the Bible. John 11:35 states a simple yet powerful sentence; *"Jesus wept."* Scholars have provided a plethora of reasons as to why, but the sentiment remains. The same Jesus took the moment to feel and release. In Matthew 26:38 Jesus described His emotional state because He understood that He would soon be crucified and acknowledged His desire for His friends' support. The Amplified Bible translates Jesus describing His feelings as being "deeply grieved, so that I am almost dying of sorrow."

Truthfully speaking, Jesus in His sovereignty, could have avoided the emotional stress. But He chose to stay, process, and endure not only to complete His assignment, but to also leave us with an example to follow. Your assignment or purpose requires you to process all your feelings, especially the negative ones. Ignoring them is doing yourself a disservice. You cannot give or receive the love of God if you are unwilling to feel.

Love requires experiencing feelings and sharing emotions. I had gotten to a place where I could no longer recognize my own emotions. Before I could confront an offense, I had to reconnect with my emotions so that when an offense came up, I could properly identify and convey what I was feeling.

Adopting a mindset of healthy emotional intelligence allows you to recognize your feelings. Emotional intelligence provides you with the skills and abilities that empower you to identify, manage, and understand your own emotions. It aids you in effectively communicating your emotions and eventually determining what offended you. Before you pull someone aside, regulate.

Resolving conflict requires emotionally vulnerable and emotionally regulated conversation. After we regulate and determine that this is something that cannot be excused, then according to

Scripture, we confront it. After bringing the issue to the other person(s) involved, where it goes from there depends on you and the other said individual(s). The goal of Matthew 18:15-17 is not to sway them to agree with you and your way of thinking. The goal is to resolve and hopefully repair the relationship while acknowledging that it won't always happen. As the offended person, you may find out that you interpreted a situation incorrectly and realized the offense was a simple miscommunication. The goal is mutual understanding. Only when the offender refuses to listen or change in ways that promote peace can other people (wise counsel) be brought into the conflict. Cultivating a healthy community requires confronting offense. Emotional intelligence gives you the tools to express your emotions to others within your community in a healthy way.

A question I had to ask myself was, 'What if giving yourself the space to be vulnerable and confront an offense is an act of Christ-centered love towards not only your offender but yourself as well? It says in Scripture to love your neighbor as you have loved yourself. Learning to love myself correctly helped me to learn what I liked and disliked and how I wanted to be treated. Loving myself correctly helped me to put boundaries in place to stop myself from being put in a place where walls were better protection than Christ Himself. We build mutually beneficial relationships when we love our neighbors with the healthy love we give ourselves. Having good relationships is a tremendous blessing. Therefore, building relationships is important.

Chapter Five:
Marriage, Prosperity, and Being Blessed?

There will always be the discourse of the prosperity gospel and how it is detrimental to the mission of Christ. Within prosperity gospel teaching is that remaining positive in thought and spoken word and consistent donation to the church puts you (the believer) in a position to be blessed. For example, Proverbs 13:22 references how the sinner's wealth is for the just. Meanwhile, Psalm 27:13 speaks of God's goodness in the land of the living. If you are not blessed in those ways or struggling, there may be some form of sin in your life. There were some ideologies that I didn't know could be considered prosperity teaching. For example, the act of saving yourself is a guarantee that you will be married, or because of that act alone, you are guaranteed a successful marriage. Marriage was always a hot topic within the church. Because of the emphasis placed on Jesus' love for the church and that being reflected in a marriage between a man and a woman, marriage ultimately became the most important goal. I was taught abstinence based on the quote I am saving myself for marriage, the emphasis being placed more on the husband than it simply being a command from God. Much of what I have experienced in the church was based on these ideologies as an aspect of holiness teaching. To make abstinence appealing, it was presented as more than just the promise of marriage but confirmation of a successful one. Because I sacrificed sex in my singleness, God would reward me with marriage. I don't think the phrase saving myself for marriage was directly taught to me. It was just how I understood and put the pieces together. Only your husband should see your body. Your virginity is a gift; cherish it and be sure you keep it intact so you can give it to your husband. Because of this, there was a growing rift between me and God. I carried the thought that if I continued to save myself, marriage would not be too far behind. That, combined with societal pressure by age 27, I got antsy. Once I turned 30, I began becoming resentful. I talked and asked the leaders around me about their resolve; my heart wasn't in the right place. I questioned and asked God what was wrong with me.

What do I need to fix to be blessed with marriage? If I'm being honest, there was/is a whole slew of things I could "fix" to be a healthy individual, let alone to set myself up to have a successful marriage. Emotional maturity, financial literacy, and home skills, just to name a few. Without it, without marriage, I wasn't really blessed. Dramatic right? Exactly! I feel insane writing it. To my understanding, being blessed was measured by the accomplishments you made and the milestones you met. But what promises are we entitled to as joint heirs with Christ? Is there really a blueprint in order to be "blessed"?

> *Blessed are those who are persecuted because of righteousness, for theirs is the kingdom of heaven. Blessed are you when people insult you, persecute you and falsely say all kinds of evil against you because of me. Rejoice and be glad, because great is your reward in heaven, for in the same way*

they persecuted the prophets who were before you. Matthew 5:10-12 NIV

If you are able to experience a healthy, happy marriage, that is truly a blessing. I don't want it to come off that I'm a bitter single who is knocking marriage. But if being blessed is solely measured by the "things" we obtain, there are millions of people, the most devout Christians included, that could never be considered blessed. According to the Blue Letter Bible, the Greek word that closely translates to the English word blessed is *makarios*. It's defined as fortunate, happy, enlarged, or lengthy. This translation of the word blessed can be found 50 times in the New Testament. The beatitudes in Matthew 5 describe different scenarios that would constitute a believer to be blessed. Some of them, like verse 10, are less than optimal situations. *Blessed are those who are persecuted for righteousness sake, for theirs is the kingdom of heaven.* The blessing is **not** the persecution. Blessing and tragedy are not synonymous in this verse. The rest of the verse states that because great is your reward in heaven. A Christian is happy and fortunate because even in the

Marriage, Prosperity and Being Blessed?

midst of misfortune, they can stand on truth, knowing that God will hold true to His word. This verse and the seven others speak of the mindset and spirit of the Christian in the midst of those situations. Someone whose foundation (truths, beliefs, morals) cannot be shaken (Psalm 125:1-5) by what they are currently going through is blessed. Romans 8:17 tells us that we are joint heirs with Christ. There is an inheritance we are entitled to simply because we are children of God. Just as we are included in the inheritance, we are also included in the sufferings, but that does not change our position as blessed. Some blessings spoken of in the Beatitudes will not be experienced on earth but only when we are joined in heaven with our Father. Merely measuring blessedness by material things dilutes the meaning. If I never gain another quantifiable blessing, I know I am still spiritually blessed. I still have peace; I am still loved according to Romans 8:35-39. Blessed is the knowledge that God is in spite of what happens.

Chapter Six:
WORSHIP

What the Church Told Me it Took to be Christian Identity

My grandmother was the type who said if we were not going to church with her on Sunday, we had to find somewhere to go; sitting in the house on Sunday was not an option. In her opinion, you solidified your relationship with God by attending church, serving in the church, and serving your fellow man to make it real. A common statement she quoted often was, "You have to learn to serve." I don't think I remember her having "free or downtime." My grandmother filled every second of her schedule with some form of service. Her profession was home health aide. She served and loved people. Of course, for a better part of my childhood, my sisters and I were with her, so a lot of her qualities were passed down to me and my siblings. There wasn't a service where we could be ordinary attendees. We needed to notice where assistance was needed before she did, or that was another conversation we had once we got home. I started dedicating my all to everyone else. That's what it took to be Christian. Dedicating all of your free time and finances was the standard. You could not be Christian and not be dedicated to everything church. Being dedicated to the church was your commitment and dedication to God. We were taught worship was a lifestyle, so obviously, serving to exhaustion, giving until you're in a deficit, and pouring from an empty cup were what we learned it meant to be Christian. That's what it looked like to live a life of worship. This was my introduction and primary foundation of what Christianity and church membership looked like.

As a believing parent, guardian, mentor, etc., you are that child's first introduction to Christianity. Kids will mimic how you live. Proverbs 22:6 KJV tells us, *Train up a child in the way he should go, and when he is old, he will not depart from it*. This Scripture deals just as much with the "how" you *train* as it does with the "what" you *train your* child.

Translations have also written "in the way he" to "according to his way." With this translation, it can be interpreted that we should be training or teaching in a way that best suits the individual child, catering to their gifts, talents, and abilities. While the mandate is to train, the first goal is to glorify God; however, training also aids children in discovering and empowering who they are in Christ and as individuals. As a parent, you are teaching them about God in a way they can understand and in a way that caters to how God created them, allowing children to delve into their interests, encouraging questions and the ones you as a parent may not have the answers to research and come to a resolve.

At one point in my childhood, I started asking why; although my mother entertained me to an extent, other family members didn't like my questioning, so they quickly reprimanded me. My asking why was seen as disrespectful. Teaching as a parental figure becomes an issue when a child has no room to explore, ask questions, or make their own judgments.

Proverbs 22:6 has been used to remind parents to teach children what is right. For Christians, Christianity is right. When children reach the age of curiosity and start testing boundaries and asking questions, the only resolution some parents have to offer is the common phrase, "Because I said so." According to author and therapist Alyson Schafer, this parenting method is known to cause low self-esteem; children tend to seek confirmation from outside sources, develop a follower mentality, and are unable to distinguish what is right from wrong on their own.

My grandmother's way of "training" us wasn't due to any misinterpretation of the Scriptures I can remember. Although I do remember the occasional reprimand from Proverbs 6:6, *"Go to the ant, you sluggard,"* to remind us not to waste time. Her dedication to church and people was her conviction and possibly purpose. That's how she was taught to form a relationship and how she knew to maintain her relationship with God. Her conviction became our standard.

My personality developed into that of a passive peacekeeper who goes with the flow type of person. Because I was the oldest, I was by birth order a leader and rule follower. I obeyed what my grandmother said. I built my identity in Christ based on someone else's journey. Joann, my grandmother, was a headstrong person, so what she said was Bible and written in stone. Service became who I was. I struggled with embracing my own identity. I did not have the space to explore my identity in its fullness until my late 20s. Because I revered her so much, I carried her lessons with me. It benefited everyone else because I came in "clutch," I was handy and everyone's go-to person. Pastors constantly doted on my selflessness. The disadvantage for myself was that I didn't know who I was until someone in an authority position okayed a person/situation, etc. I didn't have an opinion; pursuing endeavors I was interested in (even if they were church-based) always got put on the back burner. I didn't know how to say no; I constantly ran on empty, and I could not fully walk into who God called me to be.

What does all of this have to do with worship? Worship encompasses a wide variety of areas. According to Merriam-Webster, the definition of *worship* that we will be working with is reverence offered to a divine being or supernatural power or an act of expressing such reverence. How do we express our deep respect for God as Christians?

The church wasn't wrong when it coined the phrase, "Worship is a lifestyle." Everything we do reflects what we believe. I think, therefore, I am. If I believe that God is omnipresent, we will live our daily lives as if God is always right there with us, watching us.

> *Therefore I urge you, brothers and sisters, by the mercies of God, to present your bodies [dedicating all of yourselves, set apart] as a living sacrifice, holy and well-pleasing to God, which is your rational (logical, intelligent) act of worship.*
>
> **Romans 12:1 AMP**

"Bodies" does encompass your entire being. This means your physical body, gifts, talents, abilities, identity, personality, etc. Taking all that I am and surrendering it to God to be used to fulfill His will for my life is worship. We can't surrender what we don't know we have. My worship was based on someone else's discovery of who they were. God did not have me; He had a doctored version of me. I served in the church but not in the way Christ created me to serve. It was a long journey of God telling me He wanted me and me fighting with Him. I have given you everything I am. It left me feeling like I wasn't enough for God when, in reality, I did not have a clue who I was or how God wanted to use me. If we are not taking the time to explore who we are as a person, what God has placed on the inside of us, and inquiring of Him what He desires to use it for, we are leaving space for someone else to choose how those gifts (or other attributes) should be utilized. Learning who you are and embracing your identity in Christ is worship! But back to my parents and parental figures. Worship includes learning who you are. How you train a child, according to

Proverbs 22:6, sets the tone for how they worship and understand God as an adult.

A church that aided in my spiritual growth passed down the mindset that "if they don't do it in heaven, there's no need for us to do it on earth." That translated to every activity that wasn't/couldn't be done during a Sunday service, which was a sin, and we should avoid it at all costs. Whatever you're thinking, multiply it by 10! Movies? Sin. Bowling? Sin. It was a sin if it could not be done during a traditional worship service. Believe it or not, there were good intentions there. It was a tactic used to teach people to live and maintain a life of holiness. There is no room or time to sin if you're busy with church. This stifled generations before me, like my grandmother, when exploring who they were outside of religious responsibilities. I don't remember her having a hobby outside of reading/studying her Bible and maybe watching "Who Done It's" every once in a while. Don't get me wrong, reading and studying and taking in the word of God is never bad, but how much of the beauty of God are we missing when we limit ourselves in this capacity? The beauty and sovereignty of God can be understood so much more when we go out and experience life. Living a life pleasing to God and having fun enjoying life is possible and can be done simultaneously. Without experiencing life more fully, we may not realize that some of our limitations are simply parts of our lives that are being stolen by religious activity that is not rooted in true worship. *"The thief cometh not, but for to steal, and to kill, and to destroy: I am come that they might have life, and that they might have it more abundantly."* John 10:10 KJV

Chapter Seven:
Evangelism | Inner conflict

Go ye therefore, and teach all nations, baptizing them in the name of the Father, and of the Son, and of the Holy Ghost.
Matthew 28:19 KJV

The message and mission of Christ were never meant to stay within the four walls of the church or safely within the confines of our Christian community. Church growth is accomplished through evangelism. Evangelism is spreading the gospel through personal testimony, preached word, song, etc. The early church grew by the thousands consistently due to the amount of evangelizing the early Christians did. Though ridiculed by many for not adhering to the true orthodox Christian faith, Jehovah's Witnesses or Latter-Day Saints missionary communities still show the same passion for evangelism.

But for myself, who was raised primarily Pentecostal, I don't think I have ever taken the initiative to share my faith. I think I can count on one hand how many people I've invited to church, and those are probably the same people I've intentionally shared my testimony with. And I'm 99.99% sure all of them were already born-again believers who already had a church home. So, there were no intentional additions added to the body of Christ because of me. Why? A part of it would be due to the way I was raised, and I didn't want other people to have to experience what I had or what I had seen. The other portion was that I didn't think it was my job to do it. My grandmother, if you're not tired of hearing about her yet, was evangelized in the 20th-century traditional sense. She stood on street corners with her tracts (small brochures explaining Christian faith and doctrine), praying for anyone who would stop and accept it. She could argue with the best of them if their only goal when engaging was to disprove the validity of the Bible.

Of course, due to identity issues, I did not quite understand how God intended to use me, so I

Evangelism | My Inner Conflict

settled on doing nothing. I didn't share my testimony or go out declaring the good news. I experienced the good news, but I did not make it my priority to share it. My previous pastor taught a Bible study, and it was about church growth. One thing he said that always stuck with me was that only sheep can create more sheep. We (Christians, sheep) still have the mandate to go out and share the good news. I convinced myself that evangelism is specifically mentioned as a part of the fivefold ministry spoken of in Ephesians 4:11, which identifies specific people who were called to go out and proclaim the good news. I could, in turn, chill as a faithful pew member. For myself specifically, of course, God called me out of the pews to preach the good news in a certain capacity. However, what does that mean for other Christians who may not be called to the pulpit but corporate? Is sharing your faith restricted to those who are part of the fivefold, or is it a mandate for every believer?

> *But watch thou in all things, endure afflictions, do the work of an evangelist, fulfill thy ministry.* 2 Timothy 4:5 KJ21

Evangelism has been declining for a while now, partly due to the decline of religious practices in America. According to the Barna study, *"Sharing Faith is Increasingly Optional to Christians,"* in 1993, 89% of Christians felt they had a personal responsibility to share their faith. Recently, that percentage has dropped to 64%. In another study, over 47% of millennials feel that it is wrong to share their faith with a nonbeliever. If we are not intentionally sharing our faith, we contribute to the decline in new Christian converts and, eventually, in church membership. Although I believe that Christianity as a whole will never become extinct. However, as an institution, we can and will come close if we continue to pick and choose which parts of our Christian responsibilities we choose to uphold.

The work of spreading the good news has been left to those we deem worthy. In my case, my grandmother was great at it, so there was no need for me to step in or try. The issue is when these gospel giants or pillars in the faith transition, who will pick up the mantle? Who will pick up where they left off? 2 Timothy 4:5 commands us to do the work of evangelists. Although Paul wrote the letter to his mentee, Timothy, we can still learn from Paul's instructions. It could be assumed that Timothy was not naturally an evangelist, but Paul encouraged him to continue to do the work as one in spite of himself. Despite our natural inclination, there are still duties that we need to fulfill. Many of us, myself included, have been poured into by someone who decided to do the work of an evangelist. According to Ephesians 4:11-12 NIV, those God has put into a position were put there *"to equip his people for works of service so that the body of Christ may be built up."* While living in and experiencing the love of God is a wonderful perk, merely taking and experiencing was not meant to be the end all, be all. We were meant to be poured into and to pour out. Equip means to supply the necessary items for a particular purpose. God allowed us to cross paths with leaders (apostles, pastors, teachers, prophets, evangelists, etc.) in order to prepare us for the purpose God has created us for. In 2 Timothy, it would be good to also note how discouraged Timothy was and that Paul was encouraging him to go forward anyway. In a time where Christianity seems like an afterthought to many, and we feel like we are losing the battle to the world, I want to encourage you to evangelize anyway. We cannot allow what we see to push us to disobedience. Much of what we are seeing is what is prophesied in the Scriptures, but we are to stand firm anyway.

We should not become overwhelmed by the how and who. I want us to take a look at Ephesians 4:7 AMP, which says, *"Yet grace [God's undeserved favor] was given to each one of us [not indiscriminately, but in different ways] in proportion to the measure of Christ's [rich and abundant] gift."* 1 Corinthians 12:12 adds, *"For just as the body is one and yet has many parts, and all the parts, though many, form [only] one body, so it is with Christ. For by one [Holy] Spirit we were all baptized into one body, [spiritually transformed—united together] whether Jews or Greeks (Gentiles), slaves or free, and we were all made to drink of one [Holy] Spirit [since the same Holy Spirit fills each life]."*

What has helped me and hopefully you is that the way God calls you to "operate" will be unique to your calling and who He created you to be. A quote I fell in love with "The message will never change but the messenger and method will." The message of Jesus Christ **is** a message every member should know, continue to study, and spread. While the impact and understanding of it will expand as we grow in God, the message in and of itself will never change. We should all be submitting to leadership so that they can not only teach the message **but also** equip us in order to spread it. We can't limit how God decides to move through His creation by what we see in church. As we discover who we are and our purpose, we will come to know how God called us to minister to non-believers. By yielding to His process, He (God) will put us in front of the very people whom He wants us to minister/evangelize. No, not everyone will be receptive, but as Jesus tells us in Matthew 10, *"shake off the dust of your feet,"* and from there, continue to follow God as He leads.

Chapter Eight:
FELLOWSHIP

What is it for? I never used it

We've established that my understanding of Scripture was flawed. Not knowing who I was or who God was ultimately affected the authenticity of my worship, and I was not intentionally sharing my faith, even as an active minister in a church that I chose to join. What does that mean as it relates to fellowship, me as someone a part of the body of Christ?

Fellowship is the shared participation within a community. Fellowship is the means by which a community is built. Fellowship is the relationships you build with others within said community.

It took me a while to understand fellowship Biblically. I read commentaries, watched sermons, and reread the same 10 verses a couple of times, but it didn't really click. From my understanding and what I observed, fellowship was a way to get to know someone outside of the church building. Basically, it means hanging out with someone on a more casual level and making friends.

I believe I was at some form of church rehearsal, and at the end, we had a tendency to sit around and talk. We were talking about the flow of service and how we could do things differently to make it better. I suggested that after a while, I start hanging out outside of church. Getting to know one another on a more personal level versus just as a minister/coworker/fellow laborer. Understanding each other individually would help us work together better as a unit during service and promote more of a community-based church.

When I first heard the term fellowship, it was primarily in the context mentioned above. Just to have some downtime to get to know each other better on a more intimate level. I often hear this in connection with 1 Thessalonians 5:12, which admonishes us to *"Know them that labor among you."* It's often accompanied by the advice to have a

What is the Job of the Church? The Believer?

higher level of discernment so that you can properly identify "a wolf in sheep's clothes."

According to Acts 2:42, the original Greek translation of fellowship is Koinonia. It means to share *in* something or hold something in common. There are many ways we can share in something and as children of God we are united by the same Spirit. Some of the things that should share because we are united in Spirit are:

- We are to share the same Lord and Savior.
- The same guide for life.
- The same love for God.
- The same desire (not form) for worship.
- The same struggles.
- The same victories.

While I somewhat agree with what we were taught, we should get to know one another. How can we do life with someone we don't know? But I think what God requires and what we have reduced it to are vastly different. Not to make it sound like a job, but fellowship speaks to our obligation to each other.

It's how God calls us to love and serve our brothers and sisters in Christ.

There are 59 "one another" related Scriptures located in the New Testament. I've seen a few different organizations refer to it as the "One Anothers." The Bible has a plethora of Scriptures of how we should serve one another. People argue about how people in the church treat people who are not yet a part of the fold, but let's focus on how we treat those who have already accepted Christ. There is an order to things whether we like it or not. If we can reflect Christ's love for the church with each other, it will guide us in our efforts to give that same love to non-Christians.

Yes, we have a responsibility to share the gospel until all have heard but that does not mean we can forgo our responsibilities to one another.

- We are to love one another – John 13:34,
- Live in harmony with one another – Romans 12:16,
- Accept one another – Romans 15:7,

What is the Job of the Church? The Believer? 57

- Care for one another – 1 Corinthians 12:25,
- Bear one another burdens – Galatians 6:2 and a myriad of others.

Fellowship is not a blind connection to others but an intentional and knowledgeable connection. It teaches us to be more mindful of one another, meaning we aren't going through our day sharing common pleasantries. Fellowship requires us to know and be known.

Fellowship requires intimacy and vulnerability. I don't want it to seem that I'm discrediting the friendship portion that many of us have been taught. I'm expanding and building on that. Yes, have fun and get to know each other outside of the great commission mandate but also see your brother. I found myself saying a phrase a while ago: to make the church safe again. The premise was that the church is known for its gossip, and people can't get what God intended because they don't feel safe enough to share their brokenness. People, in turn, come to services broken yet severely guarded.

The one another commands urge us to make space for our brothers and sisters when life demands it. But if we lack the maturity to build and maintain relationships, we risk doing more harm than good. Can your brother and sister be broken in your presence and not fear being the subject of gossip or shame in a season of lack and turmoil?

Many, myself included, have built walls in order to look the part. The walls stopped many from healing and cultivating the necessary relationships to help us through hard seasons. For example, Moses held firm to God's command and grew weary in the process, which led to Aaron and Hur holding up his arms. What about Jesus? Even in His sovereignty, Matthew 26 shows us that He allowed Peter, James, and John into the hardest chapter of His life. You have to see it from both sides. Are you conscious enough to see when our brothers and sisters need help? Do we have enough humility to say we need help? The community, the early church built in the book of Acts, speaks of meeting each other's needs. Are we willing to sacrifice (not just financially) to make sure each other can survive? When Christ calls us to put the needs of others before ourselves, can we do it?

Earlier, I wrote about giving until you're in a deficit, which, according to Scripture, is not biblical. I know – and I hear you, but fellowship has boundaries and requires discernment. Jesus originally chose 12 disciples, but He shared the most personal details with only three for certain seasons and chapters in His life. God called you to fellowship, and in fellowship, you need to be able to discern who can hold you up and hold you accountable as life changes.

To be void of fellowship (isolation) means you are without accountability, a certain level of protection, and other myriad issues. Many viral moments on social media say not to fight isolation because that means God is about to elevate you. Go back to the story of Jesus in the garden of Gethsemane. Jesus maintained His level of connection with the three trusted disciples even when He needed to separate and seek God the Father for some things. Even though the disciples may have fallen short, Jesus remained committed and connected.

Fellowship requires and promotes healing. Fellowship done correctly will promote growth in multiple areas of life. However, if we want to reap the true benefits of fellowship, we have to be willing to release the trust issues and embrace the people God has placed in our lives. Angela Burgess, a mental health therapist, stated that to heal from toxic relationships is in a relationship. Of course, that healing is meant to be done within a new circle, but the sentiment remains the same: healing comes from and while actively in connection. Even though Moses was hurt multiple times by the people closest to him, healing and elevation came as he embraced the new connections.

Chapter Nine:
What is the Job of the Church? The Believer?

And he said unto them, "Follow me, and I will make you fishers of men."
                              Matthew 4:19 KJV

The church is a hospital. I don't know where the saying originated but I assume it is because of Scriptures such as Mark 2:17, Luke 5:31-32, or Matthew 9:12. Jesus makes the comparison of the sick to sinners and explains that just like healthy people don't need a doctor nor does spiritually healthy need a Savior. Jesus came to meet a need; without one, He would not be here. However, comparing the church to a hospital would limit the work of the church and devalue the sacrifice of Jesus. I believe the function and purpose of the church can be summarized with Scripture Ephesians 4:11-13 NIV:

> *So Christ himself gave the apostles, the prophets, the evangelists, the pastors and teachers, to equip his people for works of service, so that the body of Christ may be built up until we all reach unity in the faith and in the knowledge of the Son of God and become mature, attaining to the whole measure of the fullness of Christ.*

Pastor Joshua Smith states that the church is more like a rehab center. In rehab centers, both rehabilitation and habilitative services can be provided. Rehabilitation helps people regain and/or improve their abilities to function in daily life. It also aids in helping people who have lost those abilities due to injury, disease, or medical treatment. Habilitative services seek to teach people and develop skills or functions that they were incapable of developing on their own.

Due to Adam's sins, we lost connection with God. We did things such as daily sacrifices to atone for sins and repair that relationship, but those have proven to be insufficient. Jesus then came to restore what was lost. The church's job is to teach us to:

What is the Job of the Church? The Believer?

1. Embrace the reconnection with God that was lost due to sin (rehabilitation) and

2. Live in and maintain that reconnection (habilitative).

Yes, some healing will need to take place so you can adequately carry the gospel, but the job of the church does not stop at aiding in your healing process. The church is to walk with you toward healing, teach you how to stay healed, accompany you on your path of healing, and help you share your story of healing with others. If we go back to the original use of the church, how do we compare? Are we teaching people how to build a relationship with Christ for themselves? Or are we taking a more legalistic approach? Are we creating carbon copies of ourselves instead of empowering people to discover who they are in Christ and as a person? How would our services change if we shifted our focus back to worship instead of mainstream traditions? Would our services be less concerned with who was preaching instead of what was being taught? Could we then reduce the amount of church hurt people experience?

Returning back to the original purpose of the church and learning what it is truly meant for, I realized why and how it became another 9 to 5. At a certain point, it became draining to have to go Sunday after Sunday. It became something I had to do in order to prove I had a relationship instead of a place to help build one. Because it was just another job, my goal was not to build relationships or connect with other people in order to share the gospel. I was overwhelmingly lonely. When leadership saw untapped potential and attempted to pull it out of me, I fought the process because of how I thought I should operate.

Growth to the local church and the body of Christ would come if we just get back to the churches original design. We cannot do that without taking a good and honest look at ourselves. Growth can and will happen when we get back in position.

What's your job as a believer?

Do not conform to the pattern of this world, but be transformed by the renewing of your mind. Then you will be able to test and approve what God's will is—his good, pleasing and perfect will. Romans 12:2 NIV

We understand that the makeup of the church is comprised of fellowship, evangelism, worship, and teaching. The church has an obligation to help mature believers do the work of the Lord. Our job as Christians is to submit and obey God. Remember that your first obligation is to God. The Bible tells us in Matthew 16:24-26 AKJV

> *"Then said Jesus unto his disciples, If any man will come after me, let him deny himself, and take up his cross, and follow me. For whosoever will save his life shall lose it: and whosoever will lose his life for my sake shall find it. For what is a man profited, if he shall gain the whole world,*

*and lose his own soul? or what shall a
man give in exchange for his soul?"*

We have decided to follow God, not man. God may lead us to certain churches or ministries, but our obligation and life are committed to God. God calls us to submit to leadership (Hebrews 13:17). The goal is to make God known. To do that, we must keep things in order. When we lose perspective, we risk putting other things, people, and ourselves in a position that only God should be in.

I focused so much on myself and how I presented myself that the mission of Christ became lost. I hurt more people than I helped. But thank God for grace. The season God was calling for me was grace and mercy. The intimacy I needed to see and understand myself allowed me to learn Who He originally created me to be. I was able to worship from a place of admiration and not obligation. I serve as a result of a relationship with Christ, not to prove myself worthy. My perspective changed for the better.

Chapter Ten:
Resolution

In order to put us, the church, back on the right, we have to repent, deconstruct, and reform. Those words may be concerning for the more seasoned and traditional Christian, but believe it or not, it's all part of the Christian walk.

> *For I acknowledge my transgressions: and my sin is ever before me. Against thee, thee only, have I sinned, and done this evil in thy sight: that thou mightest be justified when thou speakest, and be clear when thou judgest.* Psalm 51:3-4 KJV

In order to fix a problem, we, of course, have to acknowledge that there is a problem. In Psalm 51, David is distressed regarding his actions with Uriah and Bathsheba. Before we can go out and "fix" the world, we have to fix ourselves. We need to be in right standing with God, understanding that all else fails in comparison when we look at Who we are ultimately sinning against. Likewise, today, there is a need to acknowledge that we have distorted the meaning of His church. Once we repent and decide to do things God's way, He can transform us into who He originally created us to be. During that transformation, there is a season of deconstruction. We break down what we know and realize that it was ultimately wrong. In everything, I believe that God calls for a well-rounded Christian, and the "formula" is found in His word. Once we dedicate ourselves to learning His word, reform can start to take place in us and the church.

I'm not writing this book to drag the churches in the mud or write a "woe is me" memoir. The fact of the matter is that as I got older and started actively participating in ministry, I started to train the next generation of Christians to be the same way I was. I wasn't emotionally available the way I should have been. I judged people who did not serve the way I was raised to and eventually became resentful when people reached out to me for community and fellowship; I ultimately pushed them away, and my relationship with God became strained because of the level of prosperity teaching I had attached to. The pain of misunderstanding caused me to inflict that very same pain and confusion on others.

I thought church was passivity. I thought church meant conformity to leadership standards. I thought church meant not having boundaries. I thought being Christian and being a part of the church meant living as a shell and broken version of myself. All of this is false. I believe that I am a sinner in need of grace. I believe that Jesus surrendered His heavenly position in order to be that saving grace for me. Because I have accepted Jesus as my Lord and Savior, I am a joint heir with Christ, and promises are attached to me. While abundance is my birthright, I am not promised a life of ease, but I can overcome it. People are imperfect beings, but I will love them as Christ has loved me. I am called and created for fellowship, not isolation; While I am a part of the body, I am uniquely made. I am called to share my faith. I am not called to be perfect, but holy. Jesus is coming back for His bride, and I will one day be joined with Him in heaven. I still believe in the power and purpose of the local church.

Ask questions

For Christians who may have been raised with a certain belief system, their faith may require a level of deconstructionism. God never discouraged questions or the act of questioning Him. Abraham bargained with God on his nephew Lot's behalf, Genesis 18. Jesus in the garden of Gethsemane, Luke 22. Paul asked for the thorn to be removed from his side, 2 Corinthians 12, and many other biblical accounts. Many dedicated and passionate Christians questioned God, yet God never shamed or condemned them. As we bring our questions to God, do your due diligence to have them answered; however, remember Who the truth is. God is truth and, therefore, will be the source of truth. We cannot allow our questions to ultimately separate us from our faith. Give God the time and space to answer. Come to God expecting Him to answer. Scripture tells us in Matthew 7:7 to ask, seek, and knock. God never intended for us to live in confusion, so don't allow your questions to push you towards worldly things for answers.

Study to show yourself approved

In each of the different seasons of my journey I've shared with you, one thing remained true: you need to know the truth for yourself. We need to know the Word of God for our own development and when it comes to finding a church. There are some who are coming to Christ without knowing anything. The advice I can give is that any person you have submitted to should always be pushing you to get to know God for yourself. In doing my research for this book, the majority of my frustration came from looking for a "verse," realizing it didn't exist, or intending to break down different sayings and realize that they were taken out of context. The version of my faith I grew up embracing wasn't founded in truth. When I wasn't getting the results I was looking for, I was lost and disappointed, wondering why it wasn't working for me.

Secondly, my conflict with my faith was that I took everyone else's understanding of the Bible and Christian living and made it my own. Personal revelation, or how God makes his truth real for you, is not always one size fits all. We are encouraged to share our testimony and what God is teaching us, but it is a learning tool and a source of encouragement for the listeners. It was never meant to become the Bible for them. The formula or how God guided them through life's situations will not always be the same steps that God takes you through. I didn't take the time to get to know God or His will for my life myself.

In writing this book, I was reminded a plethora of times that the Bible was written for us, not to us. We cannot make every Scripture a blanket statement for every person in every situation. That's how we have people in clearly abusive situations because God wouldn't approve of divorce or believing that, as a Christian, that's how we're *supposed* to live. To understand the Bible means researching the people it was written to for its historical context. In understanding who the Bible was written for, we gain a better understanding of proper application. I also find that years ago, the same verse hit me one way, and I read it at a different time, but it hit me another way.

Chapter Eleven:
Final Thoughts & Discussion Questions

Maybe this book created some questions in your faith. It may have caused you to question some things or solidified your own ideologies. My advice to either reaction is, *"In all thy getting get understanding."* I hope that we, as a mature body of believers who are secure in their faith, will successfully share their faith and grow the Body of Christ. To do so, we have to know why we do what we do. We cannot accomplish that as isolated and ill-informed believers. The church's job as a Christ-centered community is to "raise" you, helping you grow in your faith while being there to hold you up and keep you accountable. Your job is to live out that truth. Consider these questions during your study time:

1. What do you believe? Go deeper than just I believe Jesus died for my sins and

rose with all power in his hands three days later. Or is that enough?

2. Why do you go to church?

3. Do you know the foundational truths/beliefs of your church?

4. What are you passing down (intentionally or unintentionally) to the next generation of believers regarding church and Christianity?

5. Are your beliefs counterintuitive to the mission of Christ?

6. Is the church you're attending teaching people how to build a relationship with Christ for themselves? Or are we taking a more legalistic approach?

7. Is the church you're attending creating carbon copies of themselves instead of empowering people to discover who they are in Christ and as a person?

Final Thoughts & Discussion Questions

8. How are worship services you attend regarding worship instead of mainstream traditions?

9. Is the congregation more concerned with who is preaching than with what is being taught?

10. What is the emphasis on reducing the amount of church hurt people experience?

11. Is there an appropriate emphasis on fellowship?

Wisdom is the principal thing; therefore get wisdom: and with all thy getting get understanding. Proverbs 4:7

The church's work is far from done. I want us to finish strong.

Bibliography

BIBLES

The Holy Bible, Amplified® Bible (AMP), Copyright © 2015 by The Lockman Foundation. Used by permission. lockman.org

The Holy Bible, The Authorized (King James) Version. Rights in the Authorized Version in the United Kingdom are vested in the Crown. Reproduced by permission of the Crown's patentee, Cambridge University Press

The Holy Bible, Legacy Standard Bible®, (LSB®) Copyright © 2021 by The Lockman Foundation. Used by permission. All rights reserved. Managed in partnership with Three Sixteen Publishing Inc. LSBible.org and 316publishing.com.

The Holy Bible, New International Version®, NIV®. Copyright © 1973, 1978, 1984, 2011 by Biblica, Inc.™ Used by permission of Zondervan. All rights reserved worldwide. www.zondervan.comThe "NIV" and "New International Version" are trademarks registered in the United States Patent and Trademark Office by Biblica, Inc.™

The Holy Bible, New Living Translation, (NLT) copyright ©1996, 2004, 2015 by Tyndale House Foundation. Used by permission of Tyndale House Publishers, Carol Stream, Illinois 60188. All rights reserved.

Blessed. "Matthew 5:10: King James Version (KJV)." *Blue Letter Bible,* www.blueletterbible.org/kjv/mat/5/10/t_conc_934010. Accessed 7 Aug. 2024.

Burgess, Angela. Lead Therapist, MyselfIncluded 2, PLLC.

Jessup. "The Psychology Behind Different Types of Parenting Styles." *Jessup University,* 17 May 2019, jessup.edu/blog/academic-success/the-psychology-behind-different-types-of-parenting-styles/. Retrieved August 7, 2024

Worship. 2024. In *Merriam-Webster.com.* Retrieved August 7, 2024, from https://www.merriam-webster.com/dictionary/worship

Author Bio

Have you challenged what you have been taught? Prophetess Claira Smith has grown in her grace by challenging the foundation that she grew up on. Operating in ministry for almost 10 years, it wasn't until recently that she found her lane. Claira was affirmed as a prophet by taking the step and officially accepting the call to ministry in August 2018. Teaching biblical truth and Helping women understand who God says they are instead of the narrative life forced on them has become a passion for Claira. Because of that passion, she launched the ministry of crooked tiaras. The goal is to deal with biblical teachings of purpose, worth, and Identity to teach the next generation to wear their crowns correctly.

She has had the privilege of speaking at numerous women's conferences, discussing topics such as being fearlessly restored, the woman behind the mask, and countless others. In 2021, she recently accepted the *Dare To Be Fearless Woman of the Year* award. Claira was a coauthor in the anthology *Recrowning God's Daughters*. She gives details of the false teaching that caused her to wear her crown crooked and how God ultimately straightened it. And now, her most recent endeavor is chronically in church, where she combats what the pastor calls spiritual dysfunction.

    You can reach Claira via email at crookedtiaras2016@gmail.com.

You can also follow her ministry, Crooked Tiaras, on Instagram at @_crookedtiara.

www.ingramcontent.com/pod-product-compliance
Lightning Source LLC
Chambersburg PA
CBHW011408070526
44586CB00021B/2582